Beyoi

The True Story of a Near-Death Experience

My near-death experience, and how I went from believing that death was the end of it all to being absolutely certain that it's just the beginning of everything, and most importantly the beginning of real *love* and *life*.

First Published Worldwide 2014

By Marion Rome

All Rights Reserved.

Table of contents

Introduction

In this book, not only will I share my near-death experience (NDE) exactly as it happened, I will also explain how it fundamentally changed my life, my outlook on life and my entire belief system.

In order to provide the reader with the best possible understanding of such an experience, and how it fundamentally impacts those like myself who have lived through it, I'll divide this book into three parts. In the first part I'll describe what I used to be like on a personal level and the outlook I used to have on the world *before* my NDE. I'll also briefly recall the events that led me to have such an experience. In the second part, I'll share the very experience that nearly resulted in my death. Finally, in the third part, I'll explain the life-changing effects it had on me.

I. Living among the "mortals"

My personality *before* my NDE

I used to be a strong-willed person, quite temperamental and impulsive. I used to speak before thinking. I was the type that was very straightforward, for better or worse.

As far as I was concerned, people around me had better be *on my side*. My love for my fellow mortals was rather *conditional*. I was an all-or-nothing person: "I love you or I hate you," with no shades of grey. Especially in my relationships, it was "my way or the highway". I cruelly lacked patience when it came to my interactions with others and, if I realised my mistakes in my dealings with other people, my pride used to get in the way of taking steps to restore harmonious relationships. Saying "sorry" used to be a hard thing to do, I didn't like to be exposed and "in the wrong". I also had a hard time forgetting and forgiving. If anyone hurt me in the slightest of ways, I would hold onto grudges for ridiculous amounts of time. Some might say that I was overly sensitive – and I was, indeed – but now I realise I was simply very selfish and egocentric.

I was also undoubtedly superficial, even though I had never considered myself as such before my NDE. Yet, having lots of money and everything that goes with it was my life's "goal". Just like most people in the world we live in, I was in a jail called *materialism*.

Don't get me wrong, being materialistic in the 21st century is almost unavoidable, and being resentful at whatever wrongdoing you may have been the victim of is only human. However, it no longer makes sense when you die. The regrets of people reaching the end of their earthly lives are genuine. Perhaps they start seeing the light at the end of the tunnel – literally – and they realise that ultimately the only thing that matters is love.

My rational background

I grew up in a very rational family made up mostly of scientists and very down-to-earth individuals who – with the exception of a very few – believed in absolutely nothing but proven, quantifiable and verifiable facts. To this day, most of my relatives are convinced that my incredible and utterly magical experience was nothing but the result of the drugs I was given in hospital on that night of the 5th July 2011, when I nearly died. Others believe that I just had a "very beautiful dream".

I'm not a scientist myself; however, given my upbringing, I probably would have followed a similar line of reasoning before I found myself being, *luckily*, the victim of medical neglect, and nearly losing what I'll refer to as my *bodied* life. Prior to that experience, I would have given the same explanation of what rational and logical people call "the strange happenings in the mind": that it was the product of the subconscious realm during extremely challenging and potentially life-threatening events. Some have gone as far as suggesting I embark on a new career as a novelist given how vivid my "imagination" was on that night, which was physically painful, yet absolutely fascinating on a soul level. That would have been my belief about these occurrences had I heard about them from someone else before I experienced them first-hand that summer.

After all, that's the very purpose of scientific and rational thinking. It just explains everything away, or at the very least searches for irrefutable answers to life's burning questions and enigmas. Of a particular given fact or effect, there *undeniably* is a cause. What is indubitable to me now is that science is far, far, very far away from knowing the answers and the truth. I believe – no, I am, rather, convinced that absolute knowledge starts only when you die. Life itself, in its purest and most beautiful form, truly begins when you die and so does love. I'm talking here about a type of love that could not possibly be felt and experienced by us humans. I'm referring to a kind of love bigger than life as we know it, much bigger than our entire universe as we know it. So much bigger than anything else we know (yes, even bigger than the love a mother feels for her newborn) that you have no choice but to surrender and *become* that love. I am talking about *unconditional love*.

Following my experience, I have absolutely no doubt that Love is the only thing that matters in our lives. Love is where *all the answers* to life's questions are, and every single minute in our life should be aimed at giving and receiving love. Love is the truth. Everything else is an illusion.

"Sometimes people don't want to hear the truth because they don't want their illusions destroyed"– Friedrich Nietzsche

It has been hard to talk to others about my near-death experience. Most people feel threatened. By lending an ear to these "fantasy accounts called NDEs", they risk having to question the reality of their world. Well, like other "experiencers", my fundamental belief now is that this world we live in as humans *is* illusory.

Let's talk about those *illusions.* They are the basis of our "reality" here, in this material *dimension*. However, is this world *real*? Certainly, the Kindle or other e-reader you're holding in your hands as you're reading this is materially real. Yet, if you consider the quantum physics approach, it might not be as real as you thought – or, rather, as you might *perceive* it. Can you actually see the hundreds of internal components and nanoparticles of the device you're using at the minute? No, you can't. I can't, either. Our bodies – our human eyes made of *matter* – prevent us from doing so. It is, however, another story once your soul is freed from your body for eternity. It is, indeed, a whole different story when you "die". My experience felt more real than anything else I used to know of before through

my eyes, made up as they are of retina, cornea, pupils...
biological *matter*.

It's quite funny – I took a philosophy course many years
ago, back at university, and it took a relatively recent near-
death experience for me to fully comprehend that famous
body and soul dichotomy Plato talked about so much.
Before I experienced a complete separation of my soul
from my body, that theory simply didn't make any sense to
me. How could anything – furthermore, anything that
couldn't be *seen* and *touched*, like the soul – ever survive
something that was dead (the body)? This was
unfathomable to me. Yes, indeed, you have just learned
that I was not a believer in an afterlife prior to my NDE. I
believed in the material world only. That was until those
seven minutes when I could not only hear musical notes
but also see and touch them with my soul.

Like I said earlier, science is far from knowing the truth
and being able to bring answers to the millions of
questions it asks. It always makes me smile whenever I

read about great new scientific findings in the newspapers and about how prominent and revolutionary scientists such as Albert Einstein (among others who are "dead") would have been thrilled to hear about these new discoveries. Well, I can tell you with absolute certainty that geniuses like Einstein, now, in their *real life*, not only know *everything* about life and science but they know far more than anything we could possibly imagine. I never thought that one day, and within a split second, I would know and understand absolutely everything about the vital functions of a flower growing just outside a hospital building...

"Knowledge comes with death's release" – David Bowie

The religious and spiritual aspect

Just as I'm not a scientist, although I display a great interest in science, I'm not a religious person, either. I never have been and now, more than likely, I never will.

Even though I've been baptised and had my communion, I've never been a practising Catholic. I'm in my early thirties as I'm writing this book and, apart from a few funerals and marriages I have been to over the last decade, it must be at least fifteen years since the last time I attended a regular Mass at church, usually at the request of my mother. She is, I believe, an utterly fake Catholic. She practises Catholicism for the sole purpose of appeasing her conscience for all the suffering she has inflicted on every single person that has been unfortunate enough to cross her path. I should mention that not only is my family the hyper-rational type (bordering on closed-mindedness in terms of rational thinking) but it's also a highly dysfunctional and to some extent abusive one. I'll develop this topic later in the manuscript, as it gives an insight into how my near-death experience has also completely changed my perspective on my family feuds and my way of dealing with them.

As far as I'm concerned, regarding the religious aspect, I used to be what I'd describe as a hypocritical Catholic. I used to pray only when I encountered problems and had to face life challenges, when I was sad, confused and desperate to find solutions to specific and important matters. I was one of those "Catholics" that turn to God for answers only during hardship. As long as everything was going great with my life, I couldn't care less about God or the potential help and guidance He – should He really exist – could offer me.

Until my near-death experience, I considered myself an agnostic. I wanted to believe that there was a God somehow, somewhere, but the rational upbringing I received – especially through my chemist and biologist father – never ceased to make me question and doubt God's existence. However, since I nearly died and therefore discovered the other dimension, I am now certain and even absolutely convinced that there is no God as most religions picture Him, no matter what they want their followers and the whole world to believe.

Don't get me wrong, I respect religions and religious people. However, the gods pictured by humans are, well, *humanised*, and what I experienced when I nearly died and was in a wonderful dimension is nothing, absolutely nothing you can find even remotely in the human world. Note that this other dimension I'm talking about is no different from ours in any way. It is the *exact same* world, the only difference being that we humans *made of flesh* cannot access all of it *yet*. The only significant point on which I believe the various religious traditions are right is *love.*

"Love is the answer" – John Lennon

The general context in which my experience happens

Farewell, Grandma... Goodbye *for now*

Monday 13th June 2011. It's a bright and sunny day in London where I live, in the United Kingdom. I enjoy all types of weather in England and especially the rain. However, what I love most in this country is that the British people rarely complain about the weather, which makes them unlike the Belgians. I'm from Belgium and all my life I have heard the inhabitants of that country complaining constantly at the first drop of water falling from the sky.

I'm at home preparing myself for a job interview I'll be attending tomorrow. I have two jobs. One I love: teaching – I deliver French Clubs in nursery and primary schools on a *very* part-time basis, for a tuition agency. The other, for a different employer, I don't really like, but it ensures that the bills are fully paid every month: market research surveys. I am now applying for a translation job – English to French within the same company. I know I won't be passionate about the work but it's an extra experience that's worth having on my CV.

As I'm looking through my paperwork for a specific document I'll have to hand over to my interviewer, I find a bracelet my maternal grandmother gave me last Christmas during her visit to Europe. It's not the type of jewellery I usually wear but it's a gift I was given with so much love that I can't help loving that bracelet. I decide to wear it and go on about my business. I also wonder whether or not I'll see my grandma again. She lives abroad on a different continent, some six thousand five hundred miles away from me. She's not that old and she's healthy but, for some reason, I don't know why, the last time I met her felt like it was the last one. We both usually feel a little bit sad whenever we say goodbye to each other but, at the same time, we know it won't be too long before we meet again. However, it was different the last time, very different. Something was amiss. It was like I knew it was the last time I would see her. Something in her eyes was different. "How come you prefer not to take an extra week off from that job that pays so little and is not quite rewarding, instead of staying with me, your old grandma, that you never see?" she asked me, with her mesmerising smile and her loving eyes. Until that day, I had never realised how loving the expression of her face was, and that's what made me think that it might have been my last meeting with her.

And (as I will later learn) it was, indeed. What I don't realise, as I am thinking of her and putting on her bracelet, is that I'll meet her again in the most beautiful place in the universe. In a place wonderful beyond everything you can possibly imagine...

Later on, as I'm having a vanilla ice cream, I realise that one of my teeth hurts very badly. This tooth has been bothering me for a couple of weeks, and the pain is now sharp whenever I eat and drink anything cold or sweet. It really is time to make an appointment with the dentist. I decide I'll definitely do that tomorrow. It's getting late and I must prepare my suit for that interview. Apart from the better incentives and money that the new job would provide, it occurs to me that I don't really understand why I applied for it in the first place. I know I won't truly enjoy it. I guess that a salary twice my current one probably won't hurt and, what's more, we live in an ever-changing and fast-moving society. It's not like I'm signing a contract for life. I'm young, I just turned twenty-nine and I still have time before embarking on my dream career.

That night, as I grab my mobile phone that has been on silent mode all day, in order to set the alarm for the next morning, I realise that I have no fewer than sixteen missed calls from various members of my family, and a few voicemail messages have been left. People cry and urge me to call them back as soon as possible. My uncle is the one whose call I return first as he seems to be the most distressed amongst them and because he's the one I feel the closest to. The bad news has the effect of a bomb on me: my grandmother has died this afternoon, hit by a car.

At first I just can't believe it. It seems so unreal. She was so fit and lively for a seventy-six-year-old woman. It must be a mistake. I try my best to comfort my uncle, in vain. We hang up the phone, after saying we'll speak later, and then I look at that bracelet now lying on my bedside table. I look at it for several minutes. It has beautiful holy pictures on it – my grandmother was a genuine Catholic and she prayed until the very end on the way to hospital, my uncle told me.

I can't cry yet because I can't believe what I just heard. It must be a misunderstanding. Telephone communication in the African country where she lives and where, due to my being Belgian Congolese, I spent the first years of my life – the Democratic Republic of the Congo – is always very bad.

I'll call my family back tomorrow. It's very late now. I'll still be going to that job interview because I'm sure it's a mistake – my grandmother is not *dead*. I *felt* her love while stumbling upon that bracelet earlier in the afternoon. She's *alive*. In the meantime, I'm taking yet another tablet of paracetamol. My tooth hurts...

As I fall asleep, I start dreaming of my grandma and all the happy memories I have of her. She definitely can't be dead. Such a lovely and loving woman just can't die.

When the realisation of my loss hits me

The next morning, I am still in disbelief, maybe in denial. As strange as it may seem, I just get dressed, and, as I'm heading to my workplace where I'm due to have an interview for a different job, I now feel as if applying for the job has been a mistake. This feeling has nothing to do with the death of my grandmother. It is more like a gut feeling within *me*. It's a voice inside that is telling me: *"Never mind the money. Do something you really enjoy doing. Do something you love."* Yet, I attend this interview, and it goes relatively well given that I am supposed to believe I lost a family member very dear to my heart less than twenty-four hours ago.

I call my mother, from whom I've been estranged for years, in the afternoon. For the first time in a very, very long time, I genuinely feel sorry for her and her sadness affects me. Her heavy crying over the death of her own mother also brings me back to reality. My mum is not the type to cry, ever – she's too heartless for that. Rather, she's the type to make others cry. So there is no doubt now, my grandmother is dead. She really is. Well, she is dead *here* in this dimension. I just don't know yet that she's more alive than ever in a parallel and much brighter world than ours. It hits me hard, though. I just cry for hours. I can't stop thinking of how she wanted me to extend my stay for a few days in Belgium during her last visit, when sadly I had to refuse due to work reasons. Now that she's gone for good and I'll never see her again (or so I think), I wish I had stayed with her a little longer, especially now that I am determined to leave not only my job but the company I work for altogether. I have a gut feeling that I need to quit.

I also have that increasingly painful toothache. I finally call the dentist. I'm lucky. I am given an appointment on the 15th June. That's tomorrow.

You can still die from a dental infection in the United Kingdom in the 21st century

Even though, in 2011, I have been living in the UK for three years, I have never been to a dentist in this country. I simply keep visiting, once a year, the one I've had for years in Belgium, for the simple reason that I have never managed to find one I can go to on the National Health Service (NHS) in England and, well, although I can afford a private one, I find it outrageous to pay ridiculous sums of money for such an essential need as dental care. Nevertheless, I have no choice but to go as a private patient this time. The pain in that premolar is now 24/7 and increasing in intensity.

The first visit is only a consultation, an assessment of my general oral health. Verdict: two cavities. It's not the end of the world but I am devastated. I'm in my late twenties and I haven't got a single filling in my mouth. The only one I ever had in my whole life was on a molar baby tooth when I was eight years old and, during the next twenty years, I heard my dentist saying the same thing over and over again to me: "If everyone had teeth like yours, all the dentists would be jobless." To make sure I keep my dental reputation intact, I have been obsessed with my teeth for two decades and paradoxically it's been the fact of being overly attentive to my teeth that has destroyed them, alongside a lemon juice addiction that I have developed over the last year or so. I am in the habit of drinking the juice of eight lemons daily and I sometimes brush my teeth right after a glass of it, which is basically brushing my teeth with acid.

Oh well, I guess that, like ninety-nine per cent of people, I'll leave this world with fillings in my mouth. I accept the appointment for the next day, the 16th, to get the work done. For some reason, my newly found dentist will only do one tooth. I find it strange, given that I often hear people say that they sometimes get two or three fillings in a single visit. Later, though, I'll be very thankful that only one tooth was done.

It's already the summer. It's bright and sunny. People are enjoying iced coffees on terraces and the students at the university campus which I live next to are playing volleyball in the park. I am wishing I could do the same; however, the former would be painful and the latter would be hard to do as I have an appointment at the dentist's.

Lord, I was mistaken! I actually get to "enjoy" both during the whole tooth-filling procedure: the pain, and the sport.

You would think that, when you get charged one hundred pounds for a filling, you get what you pay for. You would expect first-class treatment in the best conditions possible. Well, not necessarily. Not only is the area that the so-called dentist is treating not properly numbed, but he also takes several mini-breaks in order to watch the latest sports news on the small television that is installed in his practice. I am not joking at all – this is really happening in 2011 at a private dentist in a developed country, and I know I should leave the place as soon as I enter it. This man is filling my tooth AND watching the highlights of the sporting week at the same time.

I think to myself that I knew from the start that something was not quite right with him. He doesn't look nice, and he didn't ask me any questions on my oral hygiene or eating habits like most good dentists do. Still, he has been recommended to me by my current partner, his practice is only five minutes away from my place, and last but not least I can't go on living much longer with ibuprofen and paracetamol as a part of my daily diet every two hours. Having lost my grandma just three days earlier and not being able to attend her funeral thousands of miles away is depressing enough.

Later the same day, after the surreal experience with this "dentist", the pain is a hundred times worse. I am told that it is "normal" to experience some discomfort after a tooth filling. Therefore, I don't think too much of it. I take yet another painkiller and I go to bed. I do indeed feel better the next morning. But then comes lunchtime, during which I have a very soft ham and cheese sandwich. Biting on anything with that tooth without experiencing excruciating pain has now become more impossible than ever.

I call my dentist. He tells me to go and see him, and I go (yes, I know, stupid). He tells me that the nerve is exposed and that I need a root canal treatment, which he can perform in two weeks' time as he is fully booked until then. Needless to say, I thank him, leave and immediately start looking for another dentist. The little trust I have in him is now broken for good and waiting a fortnight is simply out of the question. My health is important. I have already lost too much weight because of this tooth.

Still, that is what happens in the end. I have to wait weeks. The seven NHS dentists I contact are all fully booked, including the four I see as an emergency and who see me agonised, crying, begging to have that root canal treatment. I can't help it. It is against my principles of democracy and equality to pay three hundred pounds for a root canal treatment at a private dentist when I could get one for fifty pounds on the NHS.

By the 1st July, I notice, I have lost 8 kg, weighing a mere 42 kg at 163 cm in height. I am a walking skeleton in constant pain and all I have been offered by these dentists to ease the pain is either a tooth extraction or antibiotics. I have chosen the latter during the two weeks since my appointment; in this time I have at least been able to eat thick soup, but nothing more solid than that.

By the time my course of antibiotics ends, on the 3rd July, the pain has come back just as strongly as before. I have to wait just two more days in order to get a root canal treatment on the NHS.

However, in the early hours of the 5th July, that is it – I can't swallow anything anymore, not even water. The infection has gone down to my throat. It is spreading. I am greatly weakened and have a fever. The pain is now intolerable. It is in my entire head and jaws – even crying is physically painful, and any movement in my face is agony. I pass out and fall unconscious as I arrive at the accident and emergency department.

II. A fantastic voyage: my near-death experience

It is the same world – it's simply everything we cannot see

Most people who have had a near-death experience talk about it as "heaven", but they do so in the religious sense. They see "God", and "angels", and they refer to it as a magical place somewhere up in the sky. I personally believe that there is no such thing or place as "heaven". I must say that that other place *does* indeed feel like paradise: the immense sense of unconditional love you experience, the peace, the absolute knowledge, the infinite compassion and forgiveness... And, based on our vocabulary and the human knowledge we have here on earth, "heaven" as described in religious books is indeed the most appropriate term. The same goes for those extremely loving beings we meet through a near-death experience. Their love is so huge that they could indeed be called "God".

However, I am convinced that this heavenly place is here. Our world and that other world where we go after we die are the exact same one. Only the dimensions are different. There is a physical dimension and then there is a spiritual one, of which we can only access very small parts during our bodily lives, due to that very physicality. Our body is nothing but an envelope that hosts our soul for our time in the earthly sphere and, most importantly, it is something that prevents us from seeing and experiencing the *real* world. We cannot see everything with our eyes, in the same way that we cannot access the deepest levels of our feelings and emotions. Our soul, on the other hand, once freed from the constraints of this body, certainly can, and it can in a way beyond everything we can possibly imagine.

Heightened consciousness and awareness

The images are still vivid in my mind; so much of this experience was much more tangible than our reality. And because of the enhanced sense of reality and the heightened awareness I felt that day, I haven't forgotten even one single piece of it.

Ask me what *exactly* I was doing in the few hours that preceded the attack on the World Trade Center on the 11th September 2001, and I can certainly remember what I was busy with. However, I would probably have to think long and hard in order to remember *every* detail of my day and I would most likely find myself unable to remember everything. Just to give you an idea, I can't even recall what I was wearing or what I had for lunch on that day that supposedly changed the world forever. On the other hand, ask me what I lived through during my near-death experience three years ago on that night of the 5th July 2011 while I was supposedly "dead" for seven minutes and I can tell you absolutely everything as if it was still happening now, so colossal was the level of awareness and consciousness I reached.

It is and will always be the most amazing experience I've ever had.

I am not that body

"I am not this hair, I am not this skin, I am the soul that lives within" – Rumi

Right after "losing" consciousness I was completely pain-free and I could see a bunch of random people and medical staff getting all agitated around someone. I didn't know yet that that person lying on the floor was *me*. It then occurred to me that I was witnessing the entire scene from the ceiling. I found it really strange.

I then spotted the man who was my partner at the time. He was outside that group of individuals but focused on *that* someone the doctors were seemingly trying to revive. He looked greatly sad, tearful, worried and distressed. I was wondering why. And what were we doing in accident and emergency anyway? I asked him what was wrong and I realised that he couldn't hear or see me. As I tried to touch his shoulder, I became aware that I didn't have any arms anymore, let alone a body. Not only that, but my vision was now three hundred and sixty degrees. I could see everything at the same time: on the left, on the right, underneath and above. I must say it felt strange, but I really enjoyed it. I hadn't realised yet that I was *dead*.

I then got distracted by a baby girl crying in the arms of her father. She was a very cute little blonde girl with hazel eyes. Her dad looked anxious and I knew why. I had just heard him say to someone on the phone that his other, older daughter was being examined by a doctor in a nearby room for suspected appendicitis. It was when I went and looked into that room that I realised I could pass through the doors without having to open them, and even through the walls. What was going on?

However, as I reached the next room I knew it was nothing like appendicitis that child had. She had something much more serious – she was suffering from a chronic gastrointestinal disease and operating on her for appendicitis wouldn't make any difference to her condition. Even though I was one hundred per cent sure of my diagnosis on her, I asked myself how I knew that. I had known nothing about intestinal disorders *before*. That's when it occurred to me that I could read her thoughts, and therefore I knew the nature of the very pain she was experiencing, which, at three years old, she couldn't put into words in a precise manner. I also knew through her thoughts that she experienced this pain on quite a regular basis but this time it was much more severe than the other times. It was definitely not an inflammation of the appendix. Her pain extended through her entire intestines and was spasmodic.

I tried to explain this to the doctor but, just like with my partner, he couldn't hear me and I found it very frustrating. The pain of that kid saddened me so much. I knew they were wasting time and yet no one could hear me. I then realised that I also knew what that doctor was thinking about while typing some entries on his computer. He was thinking about going on holiday in two days' time. In the questionnaire aimed at the mother of the girl, there were some questions about the latest foods her daughter had eaten. He asked her whether or not the child had eaten any seafood in the last forty-eight hours. This led him to think of all the delicious seafood he would have on the French Riviera in just a couple of days. He had been exhausted lately and was greatly looking forward to this holiday with his wife and their kids. He also thought: "I must remember to put my electric toothbrush charger in my luggage. I don't want to end up forgetting it like the last time on my holiday to Italy when I had to use a manual toothbrush. It doesn't brush as efficiently as an electric one." I said to myself: "How do I know what this man is thinking?" And what about that baby still crying in the waiting room?

I went back to her and her dad and I knew why she was crying so much. It was because of that unexpected trip to the hospital in the middle of the night. She had been woken up under stressful circumstances and was tired. Furthermore, she really needed her dummy. Her dad knew that. That was what he was thinking about: her dummy. He couldn't tell whether he had left it at home or lost it on the way to hospital. He had already looked everywhere in the car and there was no dummy to be seen anywhere. Well, the dummy was in the pocket of the shorts of the big sister in agonising pain in the other room. I saw it *through* the pink cotton of her shorts.

I tried to tell him that and the same thing happened again. He couldn't hear me, let alone see me. He looked at his watch and hoped that the ordeal would soon be over and that everything would just be a false alarm and that he could go to work later in the morning. I then realised that I could see *inside* the watch. I could see the entire internal mechanism of the clock and, even better than that, I knew the function of every single metallic piece in it. I understood the true meaning of time in the universe, in *that* universe, the earthly one. I asked myself again: "How come I know everything?"

As I asked myself that question, I heard some music coming from a radio at the back of the hospital café. I decided to go and see... passing through no fewer than two rooms and three walls. I was now used to my new "condition". Even though it still felt a little bit strange, I didn't question it anymore. The song was 'Ruby Tuesday' by The Rolling Stones. I loved that song! Why didn't they play it louder? Oh but wait, as soon as I thought that, the music *did* play louder. Did *I* turn the volume up? It looked like it because the man making some sandwiches in the kitchen didn't touch the radio. Was it my mind enhancing my sensory perception of the things I liked? The tall, dark-haired man with a white apron on and a thin golden chain around his neck incontestably didn't turn the volume up. As he was preparing the food for the day, he was thinking that he hadn't had enough sleep. It was 6 a.m. and he was tired. He was hoping he'd get to sleep for at least an hour before going to the pub for a beer with his friends after his shift in the late afternoon. There would be a woman there he really wanted to date but he wasn't sure she was interested in him. Could he hear the music as loud as I did? The answer in my mind arrived fast. He couldn't. I knew instantly that I was the only one in the room that heard it much louder than he did, and I also knew all the notes required for every instrument to play it, even though I had never got past the beginner stage of guitar-playing in the five years since I started to learn sporadically. This was insane. I decided I must talk to my boyfriend about that. He was a professional jazz piano player and he always teased me about my great lack of skill at playing music.

The very thought of my partner directly led me to him. I was passing through the walls at a crazy speed, at a speed I had never experienced before, and yet I didn't feel any sensation of actually moving. It felt like I was a part of my surroundings: I was everything and everything was me. Therefore, moving from point A to point B didn't feel like it required any movement. I found it strange but I didn't think much of it. I was too excited to let my partner know about the newly discovered music genius in me. However, he was still in that hospital, still looking upset, and I wondered who on earth could be causing him so much stress and sadness. I then literally *heard* his thoughts: "Please Marion, don't die. I promise I'll stop telling you that you talk too much and that you sing out of tune in the shower. This is so unfair. How could a tooth lead to this? Not to mention her grandmother who just passed away… How will her dying affect her family?"

I was confused, to say the least. Why was he thinking of me dying when I was perfectly fine? Come on, I could even play music now! And not just the guitar but every instrument! That was a dream come true. I tried to tell him that, but once again he couldn't hear me and I couldn't touch him. I then realised that his focus was turned in a particular direction, a particular room. I went over there, and as I looked I was surprised to find out that "I" was there. Well, it wasn't me. The *real* "me" was up there just under the ceiling. Yet, it was my body down there. I then asked myself: "How could I be *here* above the room and my body be *there* on a reanimation table?" Yet, I felt an utter and complete detachment from my body. I really must emphasise that it was a profound and genuine detachment. That inert and lifeless thing lying on the reanimation table wasn't a part of me anymore.

I then thought: "Am I dead? Is this death?" If this was indeed death, I was pleased with my new life. It felt great. I could see everything and I knew everything. What's more, I knew I would *never* have to suffer any physical pain ever again. I loved being "dead". I just couldn't understand, while I was feeling so great, why these doctors seemed so determined to bring life back to that dead and now obsolete biological entity that used to be mine. I had the greatest awareness anyone can possibly imagine ever. I really was feeling amazing. I screamed as loudly as I could to tell them that. I was moving all around that table, begging them to stop. No one could hear me. I absolutely didn't want to go back into that skinny and pale body that used to be mine. For some reason I knew that, if they managed to make that body live again, all the pain that was attached to it would be reawakened and I really, really didn't want to go back there.

As I approached a nurse in a last attempt to get this across to her, I heard her say jokingly: "Who in 2011 still wears a *Wayne's World* T-shirt?" Everyone laughed. I was indeed wearing such a T-shirt that day. She had just removed it from the back of a chair she needed near my bed, and I remember that I found her statement quite rude and inconsiderate. I had been sick, very sick, and at home all day, every day – sleep-deprived, agonised and starving because the pain in my jaws was preventing me from eating normally. I therefore didn't need to dress fancily and my old outfits from the nineties were perfectly appropriate for the circumstances. Furthermore, I had become so skinny that if a fun, oversized T-shirt could conceal even just a little my protruding bones and therefore make my friends worry a little bit less about me – on top of making them smile at the sight of Wayne

Campbell and Garth Algar – it was perfect. I felt I could definitely do with a little humour and positivity during that living nightmare.

Unfortunately, as had happened with my boyfriend and the other people a few moments before, this woman couldn't hear me, either, and to be honest I didn't care anymore at that point. I was just hoping I would not have to go back into that body. I was finally pain-free and, furthermore, I had gained absolute knowledge about everything, *absolutely everything about life,* which was pretty amazing. Really, if this was death, I wanted to be dead forever. I had tried to tell the nurse about it in a final and almost desperate attempt. I had thought that maybe because, unlike the other people in the room, she wasn't busy trying to revive me she might be able to hear me. Well, it was in vain. That's when I realised that not only did I simply need to think of something to see it appear to me, but I could even do so in connection with past events.

I became aware of this because of the remark she made about my T-shirt. Back in the nineties, I had actually had two of these *Wayne's World* T-shirts. They were presents from my best friend at the time and I had lost one of them while on a school trip. I recall that this greatly upset the fifteen-year-old I was back then. It affected me, not only because it was a gift from my closest friend, but also because the missing T-shirt was even more hilarious than the one now hanging in that hospital room. For years I had believed that I had simply left it behind at the inn where we had stayed. I knew now that that T-shirt had actually been stolen by another classmate during that holiday. I saw the theft scene *exactly* as it had happened fourteen years before. I saw everything. I saw the way she sneaked into my travel bag while I was in the shower and the other girls were singing and listening to music in a room next door.

It's funny because, around a year after my near-death experience, I met that girl – the thief – at a school reunion. I told her it wasn't nice of her to have stolen my T-shirt. I could see the guilt and the bewilderment in her eyes: "Who told you that? I never stole anything from you!" To which I replied that there was nothing to worry about as I had forgiven her. The expression of shame on her face convinced me that she knew that I knew it was her, for sure. Maybe it was the tone of certainty in my voice because I knew without a shadow of a doubt that it was she who had done it, I don't know, but she didn't try to deny it any further. She just looked down and quickly changed the subject.

Still, I was dead and I was really enjoying that new form of life. Even more so now that I had just realised that not only did I know everything about life but I could also time-travel. The scene of that girl stealing my T-shirt fourteen years before was the proof and it was real, extremely real, more real than anything else. It was not the chemicals in my brain going haywire, like some scientists of my circle have suggested in the aftermath of my experience. On top of that, among all my friends at the time, that girl was the last person I would have suspected of stealing anything from anyone. Why would I make this up now more than a decade later? She's now a woman I barely know and whom I meet every three years at best. Without Facebook I wouldn't even be able to tell you the names of her children.

However, I was starting to feel a little hopeless. Certainly, I was finally pain-free but it felt so lonely being "dead". No one could hear me. I could now remember why I was at hospital; however, that whole ordeal with my teeth I had been through seemed so far away, so far behind me. I realised that I couldn't even remember the tremendous pain I had experienced. It felt as if it had never happened. It felt like the well-being I had literally *become* wouldn't allow me even to imagine how horrible it had been. Yet, I was alone and I was starting to find that hospital very boring. I decided to go out... by passing through the walls again.

Once outside, I realised that the temperature did not seem to have changed, even though I now remember clearly that it had been a chilly night. Add to that my physical weakness, and July had really been feeling like December. As my boyfriend and I had left the house to get over there, I had been freezing to death. They had actually given me a blanket when we arrived at the hospital. Yet, the temperature outdoors now felt exactly the same as the temperature indoors and I realised I had never felt such a perfect temperature before. Furthermore, I knew I would feel that ideal warmth *forever*. The question now was whether or not I'd be alone forever. I then recalled that there was a little cemetery very near the hospital where I was in Hillingdon in North West London. Maybe that's where the other "dead" people are and I'll get to talk to someone, I thought.

As I floated through the air – that I couldn't feel – to head over there, I stopped at a house with an incredibly beautiful garden and I realised something I never had before: flowers *live*. I already knew that they could live and grow if they got enough water and sunshine but here I could tell that they had *souls*. They really did have souls. That sight was mesmerising. I felt like I was discovering the world for the very first time. The joy I felt at that moment was indescribable. It was like being born again and witnessing my own birth. I knew now that I was going to learn about the *real* world. This must be what "death" is about: seeing things we can't see when we live in that material host called "body". I was super-excited. I wanted to know whether the other deceased were, too.

However, as I arrived at that little cemetery, located outside a small chapel, there was no one. The only living things I could see were the grass, the trees and the flowers on and around the graves. There were dozens of tombs and yet there was *no one*. It confirmed what I'd been feeling just a few moments earlier when I saw my body: we are not our bodies, we are our souls. At that point I wondered why I'd been so scared of cemeteries at night all my life. Ghosts really were a myth, I realised, and if they did exist that really was the last place you would meet them.

Still. What should I do now, I wondered? I decided to go back to the hospital. Maybe other people there were "dying", too. Maybe we could help each other to find out what to do next. As I reached the building I saw my partner smoking a cigarette a little outside the area where it is permitted to smoke. I was very surprised as he is the type to strictly follow the rules. He now looked more distressed than ever. He was looking through my mobile phone for my dad's number. He was wondering whether he should wait until he himself regained clarity before calling my father. Talking in French was hard enough for him but talking in a foreign language about the most dreadful news ever for a parent was beyond what he felt capable of. Had they finally stopped trying to save me? I went to see and on my way I saw a man covered in blood. To my own surprise it didn't bother me at all, although I never liked the sight of blood in my earthly life.

As I arrived in "my" room, there was no joking about my T-shirt anymore. People now had serious looks on their faces. A man said: "We've lost her." Another said: "Let's try again. We can't let a pretty young woman like that go." I wondered who he was talking about because if he was referring to me he really had weird tastes when it came to beauty. Right then on that reanimation table, I was the ugliest, most lifeless thing you can possibly imagine. They all looked at a machine where I could see and hear two flat lines. I was definitely dead... and so at peace. Yet, they tried to revive me over and over again – they were determined not to give up. One of them said: "She'll make it. Come on Marion, come back." And I screamed: "No. Please, no. I beg you. Don't make me go back *there.*" However, what was the point? They couldn't hear me.

This whole out-of-body experience was incredible and it was very real. It was not some dream, as many people and especially my rational family tried to make me believe after it happened to me. My awareness was enhanced in a way I didn't know existed. I even mentioned to all those sceptical people the differences between this experience and the intense dreaming life I had previously had while on nicotine-replacement therapy, but to no avail – they would just keep telling me that this case was yet again nothing more than a side effect of drugs. Indeed, I have been a smoker at times – never for very long, but long enough each time to become addicted to cigarettes – and when I quit smoking, I did have some of the craziest dreams you can possibly imagine. Intense dreaming is a side effect of nicotine patches. Yet, I was never able to "read" people's minds in my dreams, not even in the most insane ones I had on the nights I decided to go to bed with my patch on. I've never had that feeling of certainty and acute awareness in my dreaming life, either, let alone to the point of remembering every detail of everything in them. Nor have I ever been able to see in three-hundred-and-sixty-degree vision in a dream or really know the meaning of absolutely everything that surrounds me. During my out-of-body experience, I could feel and sense absolutely everything in such a powerful way. Heck, I could even *see* the souls of the flowers, the mechanisms of the clocks and the dysfunctions in the bodies of other people, as had happened with that little girl.

I actually tried to trace that family the following week but, for obvious privacy reasons, the hospital refused to tell me their identity. Nonetheless, to this day, I am still absolutely certain that she didn't have appendicitis but a chronic intestinal disorder. Sometimes I wish I could come across her parents by chance – I would recognise them in an instant among a thousand people – and ask them. Not for myself, because I know what I saw was real, but to "prove" to the people that matter to me that I did NOT dream all of that. Yes, it hurts when your father tells you that you should go and see a psychiatrist after you've experienced something much more beautiful than anything else that has yet come about in this life and that changed you for the better in every possible way…

The most important thing I learned from my out-of-body experience is that, as humans with bodies, we can never know what others truly think or feel and we cannot even begin to understand in an accurate manner the world that surrounds us. Our life here is nothing but an infinite array of pure illusions. We lead our lives based on assumptions. We assume a plant in our living room is dying because of inappropriate watering or lack of light. Never do we think it might be dying because, just like us, its time in the physical world has run its course and its soul now has to experience something greater. The sceptics and the rational ones can call me crazy; it will never even remotely diminish my belief that it really does take a clinical death in order to get through to and understand the soul – whether animal or vegetable – at its core. And believe me, I was not at all the "green" type of person before my NDE. I have always respected the environment but I didn't especially care about it, either. Now I do, and I think twice before picking a flower in a park.

I am now convinced that this very high level of awareness is impossible to reach in the earthly world as long as our minds – the real *us* – are trapped in our bodies. The sense of freedom and knowledge I felt while wandering outside my cage made of flesh was amazing.

And I had yet to experience the very best of that knowledge of human nature – and not just human nature, either…

From Darkness to Light

As I gave up trying to tell the medical staff to leave to rest the body that was once mine, everything in the room turned black. It was a kind of darkness that you couldn't possibly imagine in the world we live in. If you go to any windowless basement and turn off the light, the darkness you'll see is not even remotely close to what I saw during my NDE. The darkness I'm referring to is a million times darker and, not only could I see how unbelievably dark it was, I could also *feel* it.

I could feel both the darkness and its never-ending depth, which was empty, absolutely empty. That's how I knew right away that there was nothing in that great ever-expanding darkness, absolutely nothing. It was the absolute, eternal and infinite nothingness. I couldn't tell how long I was in there for. Time and space were no longer relevant in that other dimension. I would say that I was there for eternity. However, I could have been there for a millisecond. That's the hard part to explain: the darkness *was* eternity but the speed at which I was thrown into it was just so incredible that it *felt* like it lasted only a second.

In the middle of that infinite black space I saw a teeny tiny but extremely bright point of light in the corner of my right "eye", or, rather, on the right side of what was my new vision. It was the brightest and most velvety thing I had ever seen, heard or felt in my entire life. I could sense pure softness and life in an upper form in that light. It was a white-yellow, extremely bright and unbelievably appeasing light which was much brighter than the sun or any other light we can see on earth. It was a kind of light I had never seen before. It simply doesn't exist in our world. Yet, that light was not blinding at all but, rather, comforting and soothing. There were millions of energetic movements in that light.

I now couldn't focus on anything else but that light and, the more I looked at it, the faster it was spinning and the bigger it became. Little by little, I was surrounded by it. For a moment I thought that the light was coming to me but then I realised that I was the one being propelled into it through the darkness at an unimaginable speed – at a speed that can't even be measured in miles or kilometres per hour in our dimension. It was faster, much faster than – well, I believe, the speed of light as physicists measure it in our world.

During that journey from the darkness to the light, which felt like it lasted for millions and millions of years all packed into a single second, I had my first encounter with someone I used to know in the earthly world twenty-two years earlier –that is to say, when I was seven years old. His name was Oliver. He was a classmate of mine and he had died following a car crash just outside our school. I had never thought of him since 1989 when that sad event happened. Yet, I knew instantly and without the shadow of a doubt that it was him even though he was now ageless and genderless. He had become the energy of pure love. I could sense his love, his eternal and unconditional love. I would meet him again during this fantastic journey.

Returning *home* and being the loving Light: the Light is me and I am the Light

The first thing I felt while I was in that light was a sensation of *being home* – literally, returning home. My entire being came from that very place. Even though I had inherited my mother's eyes and my father's ears in the earthly life, I was *not* my parents. Apart from their egg and sperm – in the physical world – I did *not* come from them. Here, however, I *was* that energy. I came from it and I was made of it. It felt like that was where my soul had been born millions of years ago and where it would now stay forever. I knew that instantly.

I also felt an indescribable and gigantic sense of peace, well-being and unconditional love. That light is the most peaceful and loving place in the entire universe, where love exists in its utmost and purest form. That's a kind of love that you can't possibly even begin to imagine in our reality; it's a type of love that *lives*. The love in that energetic light is so, so much more alive than you and I as I'm typing these words and you are reading them. And talking about words – they are very hard to find to describe that sensation of love literally *living* outside you, through you and within you.

I often hear women – new parents in general – say that they discovered true and unconditional love the day their first child was born. Well, I can't speak for myself as I haven't got any children yet, even though the biggest loss I've ever felt in the earthly world came from a miscarriage. However, I can assure you that the love from a mother to her newborn baby does not constitute even a millionth of the love emanating from that light. No human being can love *anyone* like I felt loved by that luminescent energy. There have been times in my earthly life when I felt and still feel deeply loved by my friends and family. Yet again, that love is nothing compared to the one in the other *reality* where I went after I "died". The love in that realm is heightened and infinite. I could feel that love in such a powerful way – so powerful that I actually felt like I had *become* that love and that peace. It may sound crazy to put it this way, but at some point I *was* the light, I *was* the peace, I *was* the unconditional love. I simply became one with that loving energy.

It really is the strangest of feelings. I felt like I was *me* – my soul – but I was also every feeling and emotion around me. I was a single entity but also everything else that surrounded me, all of that at the same time. I was everything at once. One day, while looking for people who had experienced this, too, and to prove to myself that I was NOT crazy, I came across the testimonial of a man who used the most accurate metaphor for what it felt like: "It felt like being a goldfish in a fishbowl that you place in the middle of the ocean. The goldfish is in its own bubble (the bowl) but *also* a part of the ocean that it can access any time. The fish is in both at the same time. It's like the glass of the bowl doesn't really exist anymore." That's exactly how I felt. It was the perfect symbiosis between me and the world. I felt like the light was my twin, my soulmate, my true soulmate. That light knew absolutely *everything* about me. It knew the very core of my soul.

For that very reason, that loving being knew about all the good things I had done in my earthly life but also about all the *not-so-good* things I had done – not only to myself but also to others. Being exposed to that dark side of me and having been shown the consequences of my actions for myself and others is actually what changed me in a major way.

The compassionate light

Yet, that light is far, very far, from being judgemental. It is the wisest and most compassionate and forgiving energetic entity I've ever come across. Some name it "God". I call it Superpower of Love, Peace, Compassion and Wisdom. There are no other words I can find to describe that energy, when I remember that I was shown my bad actions and behaviours and yet felt totally forgiven for them and still immensely loved. That energy is simply love in its utmost form and I felt as if that light and its love were my *equal*. To me, that light is definitely not something "above" you like most religions picture their gods. It is so much more than that. That light was me, it was my very soul. It was everything I felt in my life and everything I made others feel. It was everything I had experienced in my life: the love, the joy, the happiness, the pain, the sadness, the guilt, the remorse... It was the world in its entirety and it was the truth. I simply couldn't hide anywhere or fake anything when I was facing that light. How could I have concealed or pretended anything anyway, since I was part of that light and it was part of me? Boundaries do not exist anymore in that dimension. Everything just flows freely from entities to other entities.

Words are no longer used, either. The language is, I would say, telepathic. I remember very vividly that the thoughts of the other entities – including the thoughts of the light – went straight into my mind. This wordless communication was instantaneous. Any questions I had about anything were instantly answered. Furthermore, I was able to completely understand the reply just as fast. I realised that I simply needed to have a thought about something and straight away I understood *everything* related to what I was thinking of. In our earthly world, when someone says something to you, you're faced with multiple ways to interpret what has been said, depending on the circumstances, the tone that was used, the mood of the person or your own, and so on. You ask yourself questions such as: "What did he mean by that?" "Is she joking?" "Was he serious?" In that world that is loving and utterly bright on all levels, such questions are not possible. The clarity of everything is beyond all that we know here. Misinterpretation doesn't exist and, should a reference to a sad or painful thought cross your mind or another entity's, compassion is a core value, alongside forgiveness, peace and love.

My life review

I have been shown my entire life from birth to my "death". During this life review I saw the consequences of my actions for other people whether they were "dead" or still alive. I've also been shown that I made no mistakes in my personal life – or at the very least that, no matter what mistakes I thought I had made, it was okay. I would still be loved unconditionally.

Throughout my life, I have done many things I have regretted. Like anyone, there have been times when I have made poor choices and bad decisions. Until I had my NDE I often had a hard time seeing the good in the bad, though.

In the love of that amazing light, I saw myself at around age twenty-two, when I had realised a little too late that I had made a huge mistake in the choice of my subject at university. I studied journalism and I quite enjoyed it but, when the time for the internship came, I realised it was not for me. I am not a competitive person by nature, in the sense that I don't feel the need to be better than others, especially if getting to the top involves hypocrisy, backstabbing and put-downs. However, the media world is a cruel and ruthless one. You have a greater chance of being a TV presenter if you're attractive, even if you're less qualified or competent than the average-looking guy with the master's degree and ten years' experience. I hated that little world where everything just seemed so shallow and looked so fake, and where being good-hearted was not the most required quality.

In the arms of that loving light, I was reliving all my pain and feeling all my tears all over again. My parents had covered all the costs of a degree I looked at with hatred. I was a monster. I deserved to die. I even didn't feel proud at my graduation and I managed to work for just two years as a journalist before turning to teaching. It was unbearable.

Yet, here I was, being loved unconditionally by that light and being shown that the values I defended, such as honesty, loyalty and true individual merit, were so much more worthwhile in the long run than pretending to be happy doing something that ultimately made me anything but happy. I've also been shown the way in which knowing about that dark side of the media made me much more compassionate and aware of these things in other areas of my life and how it even helped other people.

That's when I saw myself teaching some twelve-year-old kids for the first time, in a classroom where competition between pupils was at its height. There was that girl who was particularly bad at maths, and those two kids who were rejoicing in her failure. Their own good grades made them feel superior to her. Needless to say that, although it was on a smaller scale, it was still everything I had seen before in the media where, when you "win" something, someone else is nearly invariably seen as a loser to their core.

I took those kids aside and asked them why they felt the need to display any type of superiority. Certainly, they were better at maths than this little girl, but she was excellent at languages and at dancing, and the inferiority they perceived in her was nothing more than their perception and it was based on nothing tangible. It was when I was wrapped up in the infinite love of that energetic light that I learned that I had taught those children a very valuable lesson about respect and tolerance. I then instantly forgave myself for having "wasted" seven years of my life studying and working in journalism. I felt a type of compassion for myself that I had never felt before. The light was literally talking to me, saying: "You did the right thing. By remaining true to such good values, you certainly didn't waste any time." At that point I was "hugging" the light, in an energetic way. So many people had told me not to quit journalism because it paid more, and that I was making a mistake. And here, for the first time in my entire life, not only was I was accepted just as I was, but I was also "rewarded" for being who I really was.

There was also a review of that bad investment I had made a couple of years previously and through which I lost lots of money. I beat myself up for months and saw myself as nothing but a failure. Now I could see myself all over again sitting on the edge of my bed, crying and hating myself for being so stupid. It was a very strange feeling. I was both actor and spectator. I was *here* watching myself and feeling love and empathy for my poor suffering soul and *there* at the same time, feeling so little, so hopeless, desperate and sorry for myself. And again, the light was talking to me with the voice of love and compassion: "Why did you treat yourself that way? You didn't deserve to be treated that way. Not even by yourself." I was then shown hundreds of solutions that could have solved my problem, literally dozens and dozens of solutions all at once. Some of them I had actually thought of but I didn't even dare to try them for fear of failure. Once more, I completely and totally forgave myself, even though the pain I felt coming from the little me down there was great. It was now unfathomable to me that I could have treated myself that way, with so little love and respect.

I had become one of those loving entities. Just like them, I was now the pure essence of love.

The light forgives you everything… and so do the other lights

By now you must have wondered what these *entities* I am talking about are. They are everything that lives in our world. They are *all* the other lights. They are our deceased loved ones, our pets that have died, our friends and family that still live in the earthly world, the music we listen to in our cars or on the train on the way to work in the morning. These are the entities I met, saw and hugged during my near-death experience.

Encounters with the super-loving souls

Little Oliver

Suddenly I found myself again with Oliver, that little boy I was talking about earlier, whom I met first in the black space, and who had passed away two decades earlier. I remember that, following the accident, he had been in a state between life and death for several days, but he eventually died. I asked him why he was here. It felt like his answer-by-thought was formulated at the same time that I was asking him the question; simultaneously he said: "I loved it too much. No one makes fun of me here. Everyone loves me just as I am."

Note that that kid was a chubby and even fat little guy in his embodied life and you know how cruel kids can be when you don't fit the "norm". I was no exception to that sad rule. Just like the other kids at school, I made fun of him based on his physical appearance on a few occasions. I never knew how my words affected him, though. Well, now I knew and I knew it in an intensified way.

There was that time when a classmate of ours got a Superman outfit on his birthday. Every little boy at the party wanted to try it on and so did Oliver. Alas, he was too heavy for the costume and, when his turn came to put it on, he couldn't close the zip. Everyone was laughing and I said: "He's not Superman, he's Super*fat*," and I kept repeating this over and over again, along with the other kids, amid the general laughter. Now my soul could feel *every single bit* of his pain. Emotion by emotion – and in a much more powerful way than we can experience it on earth – I could feel everything he felt that day because of me: sadness, shame, distress, anger... I could see him after the party crying alone in his room, wondering why other kids always made fun of him. It broke my heart in a way I can't even begin to explain. I thought: "Why, why, why did I say that to him that day? Why did I laugh? It hurt him so much and I can't stand it." Yet, his soul was there next to mine and as a part of mine at the same time, telling me: "Don't worry, that's okay, I forgive you and I love you with all my being." That was an incredible feeling. His love was beyond everything we know here on earth. I actually can't help crying every time I recall this. And there was more to come...

The cashier

Right after this I felt the presence of someone I had not been very kind to when I was twenty years old – that is to say, nine years before my near-death experience. That person was a checkout cashier in a supermarket. Again, no "mistake" was possible. I just knew who was talking to me through thoughts and I knew *exactly* when I had previously interacted with that loving soul in my earthly life. The encounter with this woman in that amazing dimension is the one I'm trying to learn from the most in my life here now. I never imagined that my actions could affect strangers so much. You could have told me about that lady the day before I nearly died, and I probably would not have remembered anything of her. Still, she – her soul – was there showing me how I completely ruined her day years before.

It was in May 2002. I was grocery shopping a couple of hours before an examination at university and I was paying by card at the till when a problem with the machine occurred. The transaction didn't succeed and the woman told me to insert my card in the machine again. I said to her that, if it hadn't worked out the first time, it was unlikely to work out a second time around. Furthermore, I could very well have been charged the first time, as had happened before and which I had not been pleased about. I then asked her to keep my shopping for five minutes while I went to withdraw some cash just outside the shop. She kept insisting that I try again with my card because, according to her, it always worked the second time. I was reluctant but I followed her instructions anyway. The machine still didn't work and I was becoming increasingly frustrated. This happened on a Friday and I was a penniless student. I really didn't need the stress of being broke – and without food – for the weekend on top of the stress of my exams. I decided to go for the second option, which was withdrawing money at the cash machine… Or at least trying to.

Once at the cash machine, I realised that I had been charged twice for the shopping and that I didn't have enough money left in my bank account for a withdrawal. I went back to the supermarket and stormed at the cashier. One thing led to another, and I was furious to the point of being nearly insulting towards her and to the point of calling the store manager in order to report her "utter idiocy and stupidity". I really didn't spare her.

What I knew *now* – in that amazingly loving light – was that that woman nearly lost her job because of me that day, and she did so at a time when she had far more serious problems than passing an exam or having little to eat for forty-eight hours. When you think about it, my "problem" wasn't one per se. I had tons of friends who I'm sure would have tided me over with some food. I could also have called my parents and they would not have hesitated to give me some extra money. During my NDE I learned that that woman, on the other hand, was caring for a very, very sick and mentally disabled child. I was seeing her looking after her kid and I could feel all her emotional pain and fear as she thought she really couldn't afford to lose one of her two jobs. I knew absolutely all the thoughts that had passed through her mind when this incident happened. I felt the tears and the sadness my own words and actions had caused her. I felt her distress in such an intense way. I have never, ever felt so much pain in my entire life. If you take the saddest day of your life, the most emotionally painful one, and you multiply the intensity of the sorrow by a million, you don't even get close to this. I knew *everything* about her very tough earthly life, how she died from cancer leaving her son an orphan and how my reaction to a "non-problem" that day affected her in a very big way.

And yet, *there*, in this realm of pure beauty, her infinite and unconditional love for me was piercing every single bit of my soul. What I felt was enormous compassion. It was like she was saying to me: "Our own suffering, big or small, sometimes prevents us from seeing the pain of others and that's okay, in the end love is what really matters." And that love…Trust me, I could feel it. I could feel it BIG TIME and words can't express it. She *was* that pure love and so was I in an infinite, unconditional and endless way. It was eternal love.

Today I often wonder why, in that *parallel* world, the emphasis has been put on my bad actions regarding these two individuals in particular, who were complete strangers to me before I died. During that experience, I was also shown other bad behaviour of mine, around loved ones, and although that was also extremely intense, I know that the reminder of my short interactions with those two specific souls – who are dead in our world – had and still have a specific meaning. I just *know*.

The rest of the review of my dark side was kind of jolting. There was no time or space whatsoever and yet I remember every single piece of it in this life in the exact order it happened during my NDE, even though it felt like I had thousands – and I really mean *thousands* – of thoughts per minute. I could see myself one second at five years old, pinching hard the cheeks of my sister, younger than me by two years, and feeling her pain and hearing her cries for help, and the next second at twenty-two years old being overly jealous of the female best friend of my ex-boyfriend and feeling the angst of both of them. All my bad actions were shown to me like I was watching a film. What was strange – although it seemed totally normal and natural while it happened – was that I was both actor *and* spectator. I was *everything* at the same time. I was me but I also was the sadness of Oliver, I was the sorrow of the cashier lady.

Among those who still live in our dimension, I was the tears of my sister, I was the confusion of my ex-boyfriend and his friend, I was the tremendous emotional pain of one of my best friends when I started to get tired of her many suicide attempts, I was the disappointment of that pregnant woman I pretended I didn't see on the bus when I took the last available seat, I was the sadness of my dad the day I got angry at him because he didn't buy me my new shoes in the right colour, I was the sadness and despair of that drug addict neighbour of mine whom I used to shout at every Sunday night when he would prevent me from sleeping because of his loud music. I saw my entire life at an unimaginable speed and I was every feeling and every emotion my actions caused in others. Yet, I was surrounded by that incredible loving light and was forgiven for everything and not judged for anything.

My ex-boyfriend

I was even forgiven for having inflicted pain on someone purposefully. That was a stupid act of revenge on a boyfriend who had cheated on me. I was so hurt by what he had done to me that, despite his sincere plea for forgiveness, I decided that he would have to pay.

Not long after his cheating, he got promoted to the job of his dreams and he planned to throw a massive party for the occasion. He looked so happy and, furthermore, he seemed to be in love with me more than ever. As far as I was concerned, I hadn't swallowed the bitter pill of his cheating yet. I never would. He was so excited about his new position that he had hired an entire, very classy restaurant to celebrate. He couldn't wait for that night and talked about it all the time as well as constantly telling me that he was so happy and looking forward to going to that party with me. What did I do when the day of the party came? I packed a bag and went to spend the weekend at a friend's in a different city. He kept calling me over and over again. I ignored all his calls and then, at around 10 p.m. when he was supposed to be having fun – although I had already ruined his night by then – I told him I was sorry, I couldn't make it in the end because I was spending the weekend with a male friend of mine. The friend I was referring to was a guy widely known to be in love with me at the time. My boyfriend was absolutely devastated.

Until my NDE, I always believed that he pretended to be devastated and that the truth was that he didn't care. After all, he had cheated on me. Well, here I was, surrounded and filled with that amazing light, proven wrong – yet, in a loving and extremely compassionate way – one more time. Only then did I know that this had been the one of the saddest days of his life and it was because of me. I could see him rushing to his car in order to cry, hidden from the sight of anyone at his party and thinking of me. I felt all his pain, his tears, his anguish and his disappointment. I could hear all his thoughts as if I was thinking them myself: "How could she do that to me on the most important day of my career? As if living with the remorse was not enough of a punishment. Does she even realise how much I regret it and how much I love her? I was going to ask her to move in with me tonight. Why did she do that to me? I don't even want to go back in that restaurant. I just want to die right now."

I felt all his pain multiplied by a million and at the same time I was telling him how sorry I was and how much I loved him and that I had forgiven what he had done. That's what I felt – true forgiveness and compassion like I had never felt before. It was my entire soul speaking. I could understand his pain and his remorse and regret more than ever. This had not been the case in our earthly life together. I had broken up with him two days after his new job celebration and he hadn't spared me any insults. Now, in that world where love and forgiveness are king and queen, and pride and ego simply don't exist, I realised that it had been our egos talking at the time. We truly loved each other but our egos simply couldn't let go of past hurts.

In the month that followed my NDE, I called him. Five years had passed but it didn't matter. I really <u>needed</u> to say sorry to him and *mean* it. He sounded very surprised ("Why is she saying sorry to me *now*?"). I could also sense he was still a little bit bitter but I didn't take any offence at it. I now knew about the predominance of our ego in our life on earth. I knew that we are not immune to it – but I find great comfort in knowing that that ego eventually completely vanishes when our body dies. That is now an absolute certainty to me.

<u>My younger sister</u>

Like I mentioned earlier, I come from quite a dysfunctional family where I am the scapegoat and where my younger sister is – well, the golden child. At the time of the medical neglect that led me to have such an extraordinary experience, we had not talked to each other for over six months.

My sister, although she is a Doctor of Biochemistry (and supposedly "intelligent"), is also a notoriously narcissistic, selfish, alcoholic and verbally and physically abusive young woman. However, because of her high social status and her massive professional success, no one in our family sees anything wrong with any of that, not least my parents, who, the last time I endured an entire night of torture at her place where she relentlessly punched my arms and slapped me, went as far as saying that it was my fault. They had said to me that if I hadn't "provoked" her, none of that would have happened to me. They were blaming me – the victim of the abuse – while I had proof on video of everything that had happened that night at my sister's place. Anyone sane agrees that I had done nothing wrong and that *she* was obviously in an uncontrollable alcoholic and narcissistic rage. Yet, on that occasion (one among many), I responded to her just as violently, but with words, and the more hurtful my words were, the harder she hit me. Still, it was only in that incredibly loving light that I gained the knowledge of facts that were totally unknown to me before.

My sister in this life is hurting just as much as I do but in a different way. I might somehow have felt jealous of the better treatment she always received from our parents in terms of education, tolerance and forgiveness for her wrongdoings, of their praise and adulation towards her, and so on. What I didn't know is that all of this comes with clearly defined and yet unspoken rules. The love of my parents towards her is *conditional* and deep down she knows it. She has to be "perfect" at all times. She has to succeed at whatever she undertakes. She lives within the constraints of "perfection" while I am free.

I know that my parents don't hate me per se. They just display much more affection towards my sister than to me. I actually have a very good relationship with my father.

Only my mother, really, is abusive and perversely narcissistic. However, they both seem completely unconcerned and uninterested in what I do with my life. Whether I fail or succeed, they just don't care. They seem to love me in a passive manner and they never *demand* great accomplishments on my part as they do with my sister.

In that amazing other dimension I could see the scene of her insulting me and hitting me exactly as she had done at her place the last time I had seen her. What I didn't know before, but could tell while seeing the scene again exactly as it happened, was that she was actually in pain. I could feel all the emotions she had felt when I was insulting her back and, even though she was responding by attacking my personal weaknesses, her soul was literally raging and screaming: "Why can you be yourself and still be loved by our parents and why do I have to keep playing that character they have moulded me into in order to earn their love?" Her pain was immense.

Until my NDE I always thought my sister was nothing but a heartless and pathologically narcissistic woman (and that's what she actually is in our ego-based world) but now that I've seen the truth – because that light is the ultimate truth – I know that there is much more to the story than her false detachment and abusive ways and that, even though she pretended she didn't care, she really was hurt every time I said things to her like: "Look at you, you're a doctor of science and you drink endlessly, drive drunk, constantly cheat on your boyfriend by sleeping with strangers you've met on your drunken nights, and can't even remember any of it the next day. I certainly don't envy your crappy personal life despite all your great academic achievements." I never thought any of those nasty things I said to her could ever unsettle her even in the slightest way and yet the light showed me how it hurt her to an incredible degree every time. I was feeling her pain at such an indescribable level, just as much as I felt compassion and forgiveness for all the hurtful things she, equally, did to me.

This was the "tough" part. It was hard in the sense that I deeply regretted my bad actions. I was thinking: "Why on earth did I do that to Oliver, the cashier lady, my boyfriend, my sister, and so on?" Feeling their pain was not just hard – it was unbearable, especially knowing that I was the cause of it. Thankfully, throughout this magical journey I was, equally, being shown how a simple gesture of kindness can mean the world for someone. That is yet another thing I was not *fully* and *hyper*-aware of before my NDE.

Spread the love and be kind whenever you can

Just as much as I could feel the pain that was caused to others by my bad deeds, I could also feel the joy and happiness some of my actions had given to people.

The old lady

All of a sudden, I saw myself at my current age. I was viewing an occurrence that had happened in the earthly life just a few weeks before my NDE, in a practically empty train station. I was walking up an escalator that was out of order when I saw an old and frail lady trying hard to make her way to the top. I was carrying numerous shopping bags as well as my own large handbag and a huge backpack. That woman looked exhausted and we were only halfway up what seemed like a mountain to climb. I told her to stop there, that I would help her, but that I would first have to go up to the top and drop my bags as it was too dangerous to help her while carrying all my belongings, which probably weighed nearly as much as I did. As my soul was witnessing the whole scene I *felt* her smile. Yes, I felt her smile. Not only did I see it again, I FELT it in an incredible and magical way. I felt like I was hugged by it. Her smile was pure joy, tremendous happiness and relief. It screamed: "Thank you so much for helping me. That is so kind of you, you really have no idea."

I had no idea, indeed. Due to the fact that this had happened not long before the time when I was clinically dead and when my soul was therefore more aware than ever, I could clearly – in the aftermath of my NDE – recall that event as it happened in the earthly life. There really was nothing special about it – or so I thought – and I believe that most people would have done the same thing. I simply held that woman's arm and helped her walk up the stairs, step by step and very slowly. She was jokingly talking to me about how she used to be so fit and even used to take part in marathons in her younger years and that I should enjoy my youth while I could. The walk up the stairs had lasted maybe five minutes, but it had been enough for me to learn lots about her day. She had been visiting a friend of hers at a retirement home. She wished her daughter had taken her there and back so she didn't have to use this dangerous escalator. However, her daughter never seemed to have time for her. She had a busy life as an executive and she visited her only on the first Sunday of each month for lunch.

The woman talked a lot about *time*. She actually asked me whether I was going to miss my train because of her and said that, if I didn't have time to help her, it wouldn't be the end of the world. To which I replied: no, I still had lots of time ahead, and anyway, it was my pleasure to help her. Time was central in what she said. She kept on talking about it in every single one of her sentences: "People don't take the time nowadays – oh yeah they do, for the internet – but not anymore for their ageing parents, not even for their own young children." She told me that, even though she now had mobility difficulties due to her age, she'd always make the effort to visit her friend of sixty-four years for as long as she could because it was important to spend as much time as possible with your friends and family before it was too late, especially at her age.

What I was made extremely aware of during my NDE was that the simple fact that I had taken *time* for her filled her with enormous joy. Never would I have suspected that in the moments I was helping her walk up that escalator. I thought I was, rather, annoying her by telling her that life nowadays, with the ever-increasing cost of living, requires people to work more and more, and maybe people truly didn't have time to connect in person as much as they used to. Her smile made me think that she perhaps thought of me the same way she was thinking of her daughter. Now I knew that her smile simply meant: "Thank you for taking the *time* to help me walk that difficult staircase." In that amazing afterlife, her joy was now my joy, too. My entire being was filled with every bit of it in such an intensified way and it is a sensation I'd give anything to feel again.

The girl at the bar

The next thing I saw in my life review was something that had happened just a couple of years before my NDE while on a night out. I was in a very crowded bar having fun with friends when I went to the toilet and saw a girl in her mid-twenties crying all the tears of the world. She was sitting on the floor, sobbing relentlessly. At first I didn't really pay attention to her. I thought she had probably drunk too much. Some people, rather than getting violent like my sister, just get emotional when they consume too much alcohol. However, she was on the phone and I could hear her conversation – it was undoubtedly her boyfriend breaking up with her. She was begging him to sleep on the decision. She was promising him that she'd lose weight for him, that she'd dress a certain way, *his* way, that she'd call him only when *he* agreed to speak to her, that she'd never "make a scene" again whenever he paid much more attention to his female friends than to her, and so on. That girl was ready to give up her entire personality for someone who couldn't care less about her, given the way she was asking him to stop telling her that she could even die and he wouldn't care.

I remember that I held the girl's hand and told her to come and have fun with me and my friends instead of crying for someone who obviously didn't love her the same way and, worse than that, someone who didn't respect her. She agreed to follow me and I introduced her to my friends. They smiled at her, talked and danced with her, and even made her laugh at some point. She was intelligent, nice and more than likely a very kind and caring person. How could she not see that? I told her repeatedly that she deserved someone just as nice and caring. I hugged her and told her she was beautiful and genuinely seemed lovely and that she should seek someone who could appreciate those qualities in her.

The night ended and I never saw that girl again. Yet, in that loving light, I could feel all her emotions in such an enhanced way. I now knew she went back home that night feeling truly loved, comforted and at peace. I could see her going to bed with a smile on her face and thinking: "That girl and her friends are so right and nice, I deserve better, I deserve love," and then deleting her boyfriend's number a minute later. I could feel the peaceful reassurance she had in herself in such a powerful way. It was so powerful that I *was* that peaceful reassurance in her. I had become all her positive emotions that very night after the party at the bar, absolutely all of them, and it was the most wonderful feeling in the world I had ever experienced. It felt like her smile was lulling me; I was floating in her happiness and completely filled with her joy. I was feeling joyful in such a way that I was pure joy.

My grandmother

I then felt wrapped in yet another entity's "arms" and instantly I knew it was my grandmother who had passed away just a few weeks before. There was no confusion possible. I *recognised* her love but, in that dimension, her love was heightened to an indescribable degree. I could see all the moments we had spent together from my birth to the last time we had met and, while talking about that last time, I could feel the sadness she had experienced when she had asked me to prolong my stay in Belgium, when I had had to say no for work reasons. She had been so sad that day. I knew now how sad she felt that day, when she kept thinking: "How can Marion choose to go back to work so quickly instead of spending a little bit more time with me? She doesn't even really like that job, I miss her all the time and we very rarely meet. Is the money from one week's worth of work more important than me to her? I'm her only living grandparent and I'm old. Is money more important?"

Yet, she was totally forgiving of that and these thoughts of hers were instantly replaced by very happy ones. I could see myself at age five eating the delicious strudels she used to make for me. I could feel her joy at spending those moments with me and I could sense that she was feeling my joy and happiness just as much as I was feeling hers. I could see ourselves in at least a thousand moments we had spent together in the earthly life. The happiness I felt was beyond words. She was there holding me with her soul and more alive than ever. I then saw myself crying when she "died". I was lying there on my bed, crying while looking at that beautiful bracelet she had given me. I just looked so tiny and powerless via that new vision I had, and I could feel her tremendous compassion. Her energy just felt like that last look I saw in her human eyes. It was pure love but the love in it *now* was beyond everything I can explain. I definitely hadn't dreamed about her love being more alive than ever the day she died, while I was holding that piece of jewellery. She really had been there with me in thought. My body just wouldn't allow me to access it.

She was "dead" and yet she was there in that magnificent place, more alive than ever, next to me – as a part of me – telling me: "You see, I am there and I will always be there for you, you have nothing to worry about, I will be there for you forever." Her love for me was still the same. It was *her* love but amplified to proportions I can't even begin to explain. It was the most wonderful moment and feeling in my entire existence, knowing my grandmother was there and always would be. During her earthly life, she had protected me as best she could from the abuse of my mother, her own daughter. Through that melding of energies, I knew she could feel my pain in a heightened way and, through the instant understanding and comprehension we had for each other in that amazing light, I knew why my narcissistic-personality-disordered mum had abused and continued to abuse me so much.

When I had my NDE, it had been exactly seven years since I had spoken to my mother, apart from giving her my condolences when my grandma died. I hated her with a passion. I could not spend even one minute in the same room as her. Yet, in that amazing world, I felt instant forgiveness for all the horrendous things she had done to me. I knew now why she had caused me so much pain and torment. She herself was a very tortured and suffering soul and, in the ego-centred physical world, inflicting pain on others was the way she could feel her own to a lesser degree. I could feel her pain, her enormous distress, her fears, and I knew that it was all of that that led her to treat me so badly, just like her dad treated her poorly in her childhood. As I'll explain later in the manuscript, my way of responding to her aggressive behaviour has now completely changed. I used to fight back, return her insults, retaliate... I don't anymore and it's the love of my grandmother in that other dimension that gives me the strength to keep things as peaceful as possible. Most importantly, I now simply couldn't fight back anymore. Not after the eternal and *real* forgiveness I experienced and felt for her in that magical world, without my ego in the way to prevent me from doing so. What felt the most amazing, even though my relationship with my mother is forever broken as long as we live on earth, is the thorough understanding of her demons I gained all at once within a second. Without my NDE I would probably have had to see a therapist for a lifetime in order to figure out her abusive behaviour. I now don't do any form of psychotherapy. I have all the answers I need.

My paternal grandfather

Although my entire near-death experience was amazing, my encounter with my grandpa was the most surprising thing. It was surprising in *retrospect*, not during my very meeting with him in that other dimension. I never knew my paternal grandfather during my earthly life. He had passed away when I was a year old. Yet, he was there all around me and again as a part of me. His love was indescribable. It was so pure, so immense and, just like with the souls of the other people, I knew it was him. I simply knew it and then I saw the two of us together just a few months before he died.

My family and I were expats at the time. My father had taken a job as a biologist and biology teacher in Africa. We didn't go back to Belgium very often. That summer was actually the one and only time in his life my grandfather saw me, and here we were together again, and both of us were feeling all of *his* emotions when he met me for the first and last time when I was a baby and he was an old, dying man. I could feel all his love, his joy, his incredible happiness, but also the fear he felt on that day. He knew he was sick and would probably not make it until the next summer for our next visit, and he actually cried a lot when our holiday came to an end. I could literally see him crying. That is something I hadn't known (how could I? I was only a few months old). Not even my grandmother – his wife – knew about that when it happened in the earthly life. Actually, nobody knew. He was quite a secretive man, hiding his emotions a lot. I saw him saying goodbye to my parents and my sisters and me as a baby, and then he went for a walk in order to cry on his own, fearing that it would be the last time he met one of his sons and his granddaughters.

Meeting him in that kingdom of super-love was such a joy. It was happiness in the purest form you can possibly imagine. During my earthly existence, I got to know him only through anecdotes I was told about him, but I never knew he was quite such a loving and sensitive man. During his life on earth, he was believed to favour my dad over my uncle and I knew my uncle had been very resentful of that, even after my grandfather passed away. Yet, here I understood *everything* about this further family feud and once again it was nothing more than suffering that had led my granddad to favour one of his children over the other. I could feel the regrets he felt about that shortly before dying, but could also feel that he never expressed them to my uncle.

In my earthly life and until that very moment when I was wrapped in his loving energy, that was the dark side I didn't quite like about him, as I am myself the scapegoat of my family and I could therefore relate to the suffering of my uncle. Nevertheless, I instantly forgave my grandfather. In that incredibly joyful and compassionate world, he simply was that perfect and loving energy, worthy of all the love in the world no matter what.

My cat

Back in 2004 I had the cutest and most adorable six-year-old cat on the planet. He was a very friendly and loving cat that disappeared on the 1st July of that year. I spent three full days looking for him, calling his name – Gus – on the streets in vain. I finally found him on the 6th because of the smell of his decomposing little body. He was hidden in a bush in the front garden of my neighbour. I had looked nearby at least ten times.

And here he was again, more alive than ever. The way he talked to me was absolutely no different from the other entities that were humans in the earthly life. It was an incredible feeling. I could receive his thoughts in just the same way. That's how I learned that he actually died on the second afternoon I had been looking for him. He had been hit by a car the day before and was severely injured. He couldn't move or make any noise. He was in such a bad way. Yet I knew now that, while I was calling his name, my voice had been easing his pain very much, as it was comforting, and that's actually what helped him die at peace and feeling deeply loved. I also saw all the moments we had spent together in his short earthly life: when he slept on my lap, when we played with cat toys. I could feel his supreme joy at having had me as his owner. It felt like I was holding him in my arms again. It was magical.

The decision

Right after the review of my actions in my earthly life and these amazing encounters with those beautiful souls, I found myself again in the light, with the light, through the light, that unbelievably wise and loving light. I still can't find words for the power of that love. It was so huge, strong, impressive, empowering, everlasting and unconditional.

That light was now talking to me again. It was a heart-to-heart talk with so much love in it: I had to *choose* whether or not to stay. Needless to say, I absolutely didn't want to leave that place. I wanted to stay. There was no way I was going to go back to that painful life. Not that my life was a living nightmare – certainly I had my fair share of problems like anyone else, but nothing so horrendous that it was insurmountable, not at all. The reason why I wanted to stay in that so-beautiful (and the word is weak) world was obviously the unimaginable love flowing all around and everywhere, forever. I knew this would be my new life for eternity and it was *perfect*. It was utter perfection. Every being in that dimension was perfect. Even the people I found far from perfect in my earthly life were now perfect in every sense of the word in that amazing energy. Yet I was told I had to choose and I *knew* that, whether here in that amazing universe or there in that painful earthly life, I would still be eternally and unconditionally loved by that light.

What would happen if I "died": the pain of the earthly ones and my absolute knowledge of the universe

I was then being shown *what would be* if I decided to stay. I suddenly found myself on a beach. My whole family and friends were there crying and spreading my ashes on the sand. What I was seeing was *my* funeral. Not only was I aware that it was indeed my wish to be cremated and my ashes spread on a beach by the North Sea, whether in Belgium or in England, but there was simply no doubt about it anyway. The knowledge is absolute in that state of being a soul without a body. It *was* my funeral and I could feel the pain and sadness of everyone, even from some people I thought didn't really care about me, which really amazed me.

As I came closer to everyone – not in the way we do with our human bodies but really *by thought* – I *knew* who was there and I simply needed to think about a specific person to find myself very close to them. That's when I realised my vision could actually zoom. There was no space or time such as we experience in the earthly dimension. In our world, I would have had to walk the *distance* to them which would have taken *time*.

What I also realised is that I could think of a thousand things at the same time on top of understanding *everything*. On that beach, on a rainy day, not only did I know all the thoughts of the people present but I also knew absolutely everything about the surrounding environment: the sea, the sand, the seashells, the water coming from the sky, the fish, the jellyfish, the algae. I found myself looking – zooming – at some jellyfish in the water and I realised I knew and understood everything about their biological functions. I knew the function of each one of their cells and my vision could go as far as I wanted. It could reach what would probably require a microscope in our world. The same thing happened with the seawater. I knew the component of every single particle in each drop of water and I knew *why* it was organised in such and such a way for the entire universe to be able to function as it does.

All of that was happening at the same time. I could see all these things around me and at the same time feel the sadness of the people who were saying goodbye to me. I was everywhere at the same time. I was the universe. The universe and I were mutually a part of each other and I knew that if I decided to stay in the universe made of pure love this would be my life for eternity.

Although I felt the pain of my pals and relatives and greatly empathised with them in a way I had never empathised with anyone before, I still wanted to remain forever the way I was now. I knew without even questioning it that the pain they felt because of the separation from my body *only* would be merely temporary and that eternal love awaited them too.

I then realised that my loved ones had forgotten an important detail for my funeral: music. In the soul state I was in now, it honestly didn't matter to me anymore whether or not they were playing music. I didn't care any longer about music being played at my funeral but it bothered and saddened a close friend of mine who was just as passionate as I am about music and who knew it was something I judged important in my earthly life. His thought about it went straight to my mind. That's actually how I knew that some music was missing. I decided to go and "collect" something nice to listen to.

Not that I could actually do that physically. This was now impossible – the material world had ended forever and it absolutely didn't matter because I could now do it with something so much more powerful: my soul and my heart. Having been a massive and compulsive CD collector all my life – literally obsessed and in love with my discs to the point of refusing to lend any of them to anyone – that feeling of freedom was truly wonderful. It was so liberating. I then realised that that "love" I had for my compact discs had caused me more stress than anything else. I always thought that my music collection was a source of pleasure and nothing more, nothing less. I was so mistaken. I could now see myself back in my earthly life fearing that even one of my five hundred CDs would get scratched, stolen or lost while I was moving flats. I couldn't believe that my greatest passion was one of my biggest sources of stress – especially now that I had all that music in my mind. I could hear it whenever I liked, I could play it and even see its energy.

I realised this when I decided to appease my friend about this disturbing thought of his. I "played" the number one song I had in mind for my funeral – 'Sofa No.1' by Frank Zappa – and I just sent my friend all my love. Straight away I knew he was thinking about that song, too, and felt a little less disappointed. It was unbelievable, especially coming from that particular friend who was so rational and who strongly believed that, once you are dead, you really are dead and nothing survives. Yet, here I was, sending him my thoughts of love and knowing he could feel them – although, from his point of view, he was simply thinking about me when I "was" alive. That's when I had the evidence – though by then I didn't need any – that everything that was said to me in the amazing love and light was true. And now that I am back, I know that whenever I think of someone "dead" it means that that person is also thinking of me from the eternal dimension.

Still, on that beach, everyone was grieving, and especially one person. On the way back to the jetty, they had to help my father walk. His emotional pain was such that it actually affected his bodily functions. I immediately understood. My father was going to die not long after I did if I decided to stay in that mesmerising dimension. His pain and incurable sadness would be such that he would not survive it. He would let himself go completely by not eating or taking his diabetes medication. I could then see the collateral damage this would cause: the horrendous pain of my sisters. The four of us are very close to our dad. He raised us nearly on his own. My older half-sisters lost their mum to cancer at a relatively young age, and my mum was far too crazy and unstable to gain custody of my younger sister and me after the completion of the divorce with my dad.

The future

Although this very thought made me feel the greatest compassion ever towards my dad and my sisters, even towards my sister who had hated me and put me down all her life, I would still have chosen to stay in the eternal love. Yes, that's how BIG the love you give and receive in that other dimension is. I knew, anyway, that their pain would pass when they, too, came into that amazing world.

I then saw an image of a little girl playing in the sand, and that was the revelation. I knew instantly I had to come back for *that* child no matter what she would be to me in the earthly life. She could be my future daughter, my future step-daughter, my niece. She might actually have been the baby I lost in a miscarriage not long after my NDE, which furthered the change in my outlook on life. I don't know, but what I knew for sure was that that child – no matter how or if she would appear in the future – would *help me love even more* in the earthly realm, and I knew I would help her, too, to achieve something in some way. She was a cute blue-eyed little girl with blonde curly hair running on that beach, and her energy and love for life was so powerful that my decision was made. I would come back for her. I would come back for the enormous love she would teach me despite the pain.

Pain, indeed – because right after this I saw myself older and experiencing the most horrendous physical pain you can imagine. I knew now that I would "die" under particularly difficult circumstances and yet I thought the love of that child was worth the pain. My decision was made. "I'll go back to that painful world. I'm not scared anymore anyway. I will never be scared of anything ever again, least of all 'death'." The reason I came back is love. I need to love more. I need to make others love more so that they experience the best of their afterlife and they don't have to see too much of pain they have inflicted on others like I did with Oliver, the cashier lady, my ex-boyfriend and so many more.

The return to my body

As the very thought of accepting the return to this life crossed my mind, I was thrown back into that tunnel at the same speed I had entered it, and the return to my actual body was the most painful thing I have ever experienced. It felt like trying to fit a giant hand into a baby glove. It felt tight and very uncomfortable. I could hear everything of the biological matter that body is made of. I could hear the noise of every single cell in it, the water, the blood circulating, my heart pumping so loudly. And finally I could feel the tremendous physical pain in my jaws and now in my torso from the resuscitation work.

I was awake. I mean, my body was awake but everything around me now just looked and felt like an illusion. All these people around me couldn't be real after that higher, much higher form of reality I had just experienced. The doctor said to me: "Well done, Marion, you're a fighter. You're coming back from afar. We nearly lost you. You were completely unconscious for seven minutes." I thought: "Seven minutes? Really? I just lived for eternity."

I was angry – incredibly disappointed. I asked him why he had done that to me when I had repeatedly told him and his team to leave me alone. He looked confused: "What do you mean by leaving you alone?" I then explained to him that I had told him several times to leave me to die, that I was fine, but he wouldn't listen to me.

I insisted I had screamed at him to stop trying so hard to revive me and that if he didn't believe me he could ask the nurse who made jokes about my *Wayne's World* T-shirt, at which he giggled. He then went pale, very pale, with his eyes wide open in disbelief. "You could not have heard that, you were clinically dead for seven minutes," he said. "You were already unconscious when you arrived in this room and we took your T-shirt off." He then turned to the nurse and I said, "Yes, it's her, she was the one joking about my T-shirt," and to make sure he was right he asked her very quietly whether she had mentioned my T-shirt again in the moments since I woke up. She was not sure.

She looked just as stunned and petrified as he did that I could have heard that.

I then realised instinctively that I should not talk anymore, at least not to *them*. Yet, I knew that everything I had felt and seen was real. It was much more real, a million times more real than those people around me in that room.

I stayed there for a few extra hours. I asked them if I could go "for a walk" and they said no because I was still too weak. The truth is, I didn't really want to go for a walk. It wasn't the reason why I wanted to get out of that bed. I wanted to find the kitchen where I *had seen* that man listening to the Rolling Stones on the radio and thinking of the drink he would have with his friends after his shift. I asked my boyfriend if he could wander near to that kitchen and try to see the very tall, black-haired and brown-eyed cook with a very thin golden chain around his neck. He refused because "We didn't go near any kitchen when we arrived at the hospital and it must have been a dream you had, like the doctor just said."

From the very moment he said that, I knew deep down it was over between us. I knew he would never understand me ever again and that we had just become the worst match you could possibly find. Couples face incompatibilities in their relationship that can more or less be overcome or overlooked, and I've always been rather tolerant in my love life. However, this was now a *major* incompatibility with my newly found ultimate values in life. It was no longer a matter of one loving jazz and the other rock music. It was no longer a matter of one being fond of horror films and the other crazy about psychological thrillers, or one being an early bird and the other a night owl. It was now an incompatibility on a *profound soul level*.

On the way home after I was finally discharged from the hospital, we drove past the cemetery and I asked to turn around. There was something in the front garden of a house located in a street nearby I absolutely needed to see. I needed to see those flowers, those purple flowers with *souls* living brightly in them. By this point, not only was my ex-boyfriend exhausted because of his sleepless night but he was also getting seriously exasperated by the recalling of my "dreams and visions". However, I insisted. I promised him we would find the house quickly because I *knew exactly* where it was. And indeed I did, and the flowers were there. I recognised the house instantly. I simply smiled. I couldn't see their souls anymore but I knew it was just a matter of time before I could again, and next time I'd live with their love forever.

III. What now?

The silence

Following that incredible experience, I simply didn't speak for a week. People around me thought that it was because of the root canal treatment I finally managed to get done two days later at the practice of another private dentist (my faith in NHS dentists was forever lost), who would become one of my best friends for the next two and a half years until he retired. However, it wasn't that. The nerve in that tooth had now gone and mild painkillers did the job of handling the discomfort that now just seemed like a joke compared to the agony I had experienced forty-eight hours earlier.

I was silent simply because I couldn't handle the teasing about my "beautiful dreams" anymore from the very people who were supposed to support me. I was just thinking a lot. For the first time in my life, I had become a true *believer*. It was life-changing indeed.

The guilt

How could you possibly look into the eyes of your friends and family when you had chosen love over them? How could you possibly tell them that you hadn't wanted to come back, and preferred to be "dead" and this in the name of love…?

My friends and family know only the earthly form of love. They wouldn't understand what I really mean by "love", that infinite and far more powerful kind I felt in the light.

The conflicting emotions I was now facing every minute of my existence in the aftermath of my NDE were unbearable. Because that magnificent light had given me the choice of whether or not to stay in that amazing and beautiful dimension, and I had chosen to remain forever in its energy of pure love, even though I knew the pain this was going to cause to my loved ones in *an earthly way*, I couldn't help but feel guilty.

Indeed, who could possibly understand that, here among humans? That colossal love I felt in that parallel universe doesn't exist here. Except for someone who has lived the same experience, absolutely no one could grasp even a millionth of what it felt to be unconditionally loved. The word *unconditional* in the human language doesn't reflect even remotely what it meant among those loving beings I met.

To make matters worse, I am mostly surrounded by sceptical people. No one in my family believes that my experience was real, and even more real than all the so-called facts proven by science. My most rational friends keep saying that I more than likely dreamed all of that. I have no one to talk to about that incredible love, that compassion beyond words and that forgiveness in the purest form you can find. These can hardly be understood by humans in their own earthly dimension so how can these men and women even begin to fathom what it feels like in the afterlife where those feelings are so powerful that you actually become the essence of them?

How could they possibly understand that, with so much powerful love all around me and in me, it was actually only human to want to stay *there* as opposed to coming back *here* to this painful realm where nothing seems real anymore to me. The world now seems more illusory than ever. When I came back I felt so lonely among these "mortals" and yet so at peace at the same time. But I *know* I'll find my way. That light I saw was the truth. That amazing being certainly didn't lie to me and I know that I came back with some of its energy and I now have to learn to use it on earth.

Have I become religious?

If love can be classified as a religion, YES I have. If you're referring to the man-made religions as we know them, NO I haven't. However, I must admit that there are many similarities between the light I saw and God as most religions picture Him. In both cases it's a being of unconditional love. Where I disagree with religions, though, concerns the way they portray that supreme entity as *above* everything else. However, the energetic light was nothing superior to me. It was literally my *equal*. It was all my emotions, all my life, all my soul. It was all the other entities. We were all ONE and all equal. Furthermore, if Hell exists, like many religions make their followers believe, and if it is God that sends "lost" souls to that horrendous place, the Light simply cannot be called and viewed as "God" in the religious sense. There is simply no way, and I mean it REALLY IS IMPOSSIBLE that that all-loving and compassionate light would send *anyone* to a place where souls are promised agony for eternity. That light is far too compassionate and forgiving for that and it wants nothing but the very highest good for you.

No more fears, and being true to myself

Would you believe it but, as I was writing this book – just when I was halfway through it – that tooth that nearly killed me three years ago broke and this time could not be saved! I am getting a dental implant. Anyone that had gone through the ordeal I went through that summer of 2011 because of my dental problems would usually go into panic mode and die of fear. Well, I am taking it very philosophically and, better than that, I am not scared. Nothing can go wrong. Yes, the extraction of that tooth was unpleasant; yes, it hurt like hell when the anaesthetic wore off; and no, it's not nice to eat porridge and mashed potatoes only, on only one side of the mouth. All of that is *temporary*, though.

That is the greatest thing about the earthly life: *time*. Whatever pain we experience, whether physical or emotional, will only last for a certain time. And when you compare time to eternity – that feeling of eternity I felt in that mesmerising light – everything suddenly feels very, very trivial, including suffering and especially suffering. I know now that all the painful moments I experience *here* will all vanish in an instant when my soul leaves my body and is replaced with a type of well-being we can't even begin to imagine, but this time for eternity.

In the same way that I don't fear pain anymore, I don't fear "making mistakes", either, as long as those "mistakes" serve what my heart truly needs and the joy it can bring to others. In the month following my NDE, I kept thinking again and over again of my last physical meeting with my grandmother and her amazing love in the Light. Now I really couldn't understand why I had indeed chosen to go back to work instead of spending an extra week with her during her holiday in Europe. Why did I let work and furthermore a job I didn't like prevent me from having the last hugs and laughter I could have shared with my grandma before she died, and that would have made us both feel so *happy*? Is money that important compared to happiness?

My decision was made. I left my job soon afterwards, including the one I had not even started yet, and I faced the biggest fear I had prior to my NDE: *going it alone* by starting my French Club business. I can't count the number of people who told me: "Marion, you're crazy. Being self-employed in this economy is insane. There is no security, no prospects for a good pension..."

Nothing and no one could have stopped me. My fear had now vanished. I *had to* start living a life truer to myself. After my near-death experience, it felt vital to do that. I now run a small business delivering French Clubs, and not only was it the best "mistake" I ever made, because it's not hard to get up to go to work anymore, but most importantly it's a job that brings *joy* to others. No corporate job could ever replace the "Bonjour!", said with lots of enthusiasm, and smiling faces of the children that I teach every morning. Furthermore, it allows me to work part-time only and still live decently. I now have more time to dedicate to the people that I love and this, too, is priceless, and worth much more than the many extra hours I spent in offices in the past and which caused me to cancel and miss out on so many cups of tea and nice moments I could have had with my friends instead. An hour in a café with a friend, a walk in the park with my elderly neighbour, a film at the cinema with my pals, listening to a depressed friend... These are the things where I now put most of my energy. The feelings you experience through these actions, as insignificant as they may seem here on earth, *are* the *real life*. The extra sales you do at work after 5 p.m. are not.

I now live for love, joy and happiness and I don't fear anything anymore, let alone "death". After such an experience I know that no such thing as death exists – quite the opposite. You reach such a level of awareness and consciousness that you actually feel a million times more *alive*. So much so that I believe that the term near-death experience should be renamed *Real-Life Experience*.

"Death may be the greatest of all human blessings" – *Socrates*

Being wiser and living for love

One thing that has changed since my NDE is that I now try to direct that love more <u>wisely</u>. In our ego-based earthly life, conflicts are inevitable, just as much as hatred. However, we have a choice between love and hatred. I choose love, genuine love. Love is now my ultimate goal in life. It really feels like I have brought back a little bit of that amazing loving light's energy with me to earth. I value love in a way I didn't before.

That is the reason why I cut all ties with quite a number of people following that experience. I now have a better ability to recognise authentic love and that's now the very type of love I live for. Shallowness is not something I can live with anymore. I nurture the relationships that are truly based on love and I completely let go of the superficial ones, even more so if they don't bring anything truly positive. Our time here is limited. However, the time we spend on earth is our future in the afterlife. That's the reason why I truly believe that we should put all our focus on happiness – both the happiness we bring to ourselves, but even more so the happiness we give to other people.

Through my NDE I figured out that anything we do to others we ultimately do to ourselves once we access that other amazing dimension. However, over there, we experience it in a much more powerful way and that's the reason why I believe we'd better do something good. Believe it or not, I think of my encounter with Oliver in that magical world nearly every day. Maybe that one affects me more than the others because I made him suffer while he was an innocent child. Yet, even though I was totally forgiven both by him and the light, I could still feel his pain – and not like we feel emotions here, but in an enhanced way that was *particularly painful to me*. As much as the joy felt especially joyful, the emotional pain felt, equally, extremely painful. My NDE made me understand the true meaning of life and of human relations.

We get what we give and what we allow ourselves to receive, and it had better be love.

Certainly, I can't be loved by everyone, and equally I can't love everyone else. Some people don't like me and there are some people I don't like. However, instead of fighting and quarrelling, I now just walk away. If it involves tensions, even in the smallest form, that might potentially hurt me or someone else, I don't try to prove my point anymore. I simply say "let's move on," "I wish you to be happy," and I leave it at that. I choose peace over a battle of egos. I literally have nothing to gain from putting any energy into anything negative, because, whether I am the initiator of these negative things or someone else is, I will ultimately feel everything from both sides at once when I die.

I believe that if I hadn't had that near-death experience, I would have been fighting with my mother for the rest of our lives. I could be particularly feisty with her. She's the most crazy-making person you can find on the planet and I used to fight back against every single one of her attacks. That is now something I avoid as much as I can and I do it in the name of love. Not the love that I feel for her here on earth – sadly, that one died through a lifetime of emotional abuse on her part. I do it for the love I have for her but which I cannot see yet – the unconditional love I will feel for her in the afterlife.

If I am hurt by her again, or anyone else, I now make the very conscious choice not to hurt them back because I am much more aware of the effect every single one of my words and actions will have on others on a deep soul level, and also because I now know with absolute certainty that ultimately it's me that I am hurting in an unimaginable way from a human perspective.

Don't get me wrong, I still fail at it sometimes – I regained my human body, after all. However, I recognise and own up to my mistakes much more easily than I used to prior to my NDE. And when I say sorry it comes from the very depths of my heart and soul.

No more regrets for having loved some people "undeserving" of my love

Even though I was and probably still am – although to a much lesser degree – the ego-centred and selfish human being I described at the beginning of this book, I have nonetheless been a very loving and caring person, too, to the people that have mattered to me. So much so that I have even sometimes been described as "naive", and this might be right to some extent given the time it took me to break free from my sister's and mother's abuse... Despite the many fights, I tried for years to mend bridges and I tried to do so from a place of love. Other people would certainly not have waited until their thirties to walk away from such negative folk – or from other dishonest individuals, on the few occasions I had believed in the "love" of some men who later showed through their actions that they didn't really care about me.

I can't count the number of times I have accepted the unacceptable and forgiven the unforgivable *from a human point of view*. I often remained that loving person through the most horrible situations. People who cared about me couldn't understand how I could possibly keep loving some people who did nothing but disrespect and walk all over me. Well, the reason was just that: *love.* Certainly, many times I have regretted giving my love to people who didn't deserve it in the human definition of *being deserving*. Now, however – and more than ever since my experience – I don't regret it anymore, and if I had to do it all over again, I would.

I have become even more forgiving and so much more compassionate. My ability to forgive has now become considerably more genuine and stems from a deep sense of selflessness and altruism. My NDE has proven to me that this life is nothing but an illusion, so what do I truly know about the real thoughts and feelings of others? What do I really know about their motives for treating me badly or with care and love? I know nothing and, when in doubt, I will now always give love a chance. Always.

I am learning to have much more patience when it comes to my dealings with others. Where I used to get all fired up about everything and nothing, I now pause for a minute and think about what might cause other people to act in a rude or hurtful manner. Who knows what's really going on in the depths of their souls? Maybe they are hurting, and hurt often comes from a place of love. There is therefore no point in getting angry or being resentful. Sending vibes of peace and love seems now to me much more appropriate than it was before.

In the magnificent energy of that super-loving light I understood that love is the only thing that matters and that love is *everywhere:* a smile to a stranger who looks sad, a compliment to your boss or your colleague, a kind word to a friend who is going through a difficult time, or even for no particular reason... These things seem like nothing in our daily interactions but it's simply because we cannot see the true meaning of life yet. Our bodies won't allow us to. However, it means a lot, on a deep soul level, once we reach that other dimension where love rules for eternity.

"The soul of man is immortal and imperishable" – Plato

Thank you very much for reading *Beyond Sight*. Whatever your reason for choosing this book, I hope you found some answers to at least some of your questions about near-death experiences. However, *Beyond Sight* is more than just an NDE tale: the effects this experience has had on my life have been massively positive. In my follow-up book, *Through the Light*, I explain how my meeting with the Light has transformed my life on pretty much all levels and how it has led me to develop an unshakeable optimism about human nature as well as a very idealistic vision of love.

Know that you are immensely loved by a force much greater than all that we know in the earthly realm. That eternal, space-less, timeless, ever-expanding and incredibly beautiful world I saw is very much alive *right here, right now*. Therefore, whoever you are and wherever you are, I already love you.

Marion

Made in the USA
Lexington, KY
28 October 2016